LUCINDA'S

RUSTIC ITALIAN KITCHEN

LUCINDA'S
RUSTIC ITALIAN KITCHEN

LUCINDA SCALA QUINN · PHOTOGRAPHS BY QUENTIN BACON

BICENTENNIAL
1807
WILEY
2007
BICENTENNIAL

JOHN WILEY & SONS, INC.

Published by John Wiley & Sons, Inc., Hoboken, New Jersey
Published simultaneously in Canada

For general information about our other products and services, please contact our Customer Care Department within the United States at (800) 762-2974, outside the United States at (317) 572-3993 or fax (317) 572-4002.

Wiley also publishes its books in a variety of electronic formats. Some content that appears in print may not be available in electronic books. For more information about Wiley products, visit our web site at www.wiley.com.

Library of Congress Cataloging-in-Publication Data:

Quinn, Lucinda Scala.
  Lucinda's rustic Italian kitchen / Lucinda Scala Quinn.
     p. cm.
  Includes bibliographical references and index.
  ISBN-13: 978-0-471-79381-6 (cloth)
  1. Cookery, Italian. I. Title.

  TX723.Q56 2007
  641.5945—dc22
                              2006010289

Printed in China

10 9 8 7 6 5 4 3 2 1

FOR MY DAD
CARMINE GEORGE SCALA

CONTENTS

ACKNOWLEDGMENTS

I am eternally grateful to Martha Stewart, who has given me more opportunites than any cook could hope for. Thank you, Martha, and all my colleagues at MSLO, for continually teaching and inspiring me every day. Thank you Carla Glasser and Justin Schwartz. You gave my dream to write books a chance. Uncle Jim and Aunt Lucia safeguarded the family recipe files and shared them with me. To all my cousins—I hope you find something within to spark your own memories. Our old-time, multi-generational family gatherings live cinematically in my mind.

I am fortunate to have been raised in a family where the simple act of gathering together at the family table for meals was a highly valued routine, one that allowed for the daily exchange of thoughts, feelings, emotions and fundamental nourishment. Love and thanks to my parents, Rosemary and George Scala. Today, my brothers, Jim, David and Peter, and I continue the tradition with our own families.

Richard, Calder, Miles and Luca, I love you forever.

INTRODUCTION

This is the food of my heart and soul. Most of my warm family memories are inextricably and forever linked to Italian food. This humble volume of simple-to-prepare recipes is culled from my family's personal collection. It combines tastes from my Italian-American childhood with flavors remembered over years of visiting Italy. Be it a weeknight supper or a languorous Sunday dinner, the Italians know that there is goodness to gain from the rituals that lay within a carefully made meal shared with family and friends.

From early childhood, I remember being perched on my grandmother's knee, as she argued with her sister-in-law over the proper technique for cooking meatballs; the Scalas browned them first, the Ferlos dropped the raw meatballs into the bubbling hot tomato sauce. Their lasagna had miniature meatballs tucked between its layers, and those same little jewels could be found floating in a bowl of escarole soup.

My great-grand-parents Thomas and Aqualina Ferlo, Rome, New York.

I recorded my Italian family history many years ago in a photographic documentary titled *Five Sisters from Rome, New York*, about my paternal grandmother, Mary Ferlo

Scala, and her sisters, Elizabeth (Bessy), Valentine (Wally), Sara and Jane. Every story was shared while we prepared and ate meals together. The sisters' legacy along with that of their mother, Aqualina, daughter of my great-great-grandmother, Archangela Spadafore, is a powerful snapshot of Italian-American immigrant women and their rituals, which centered around the family table.

My dad's sister, Aunt Gina, remembered her grandmother, Aqualina. "My grandmother was a very forceful woman. When people came from the old country, Grandpa

Aqualina on her wedding day.

would sponsor them. He used to send her to New York City to meet the boat. She was a great woman who knew a little about a lot of things. She was the business head in the family. When she was young, she was beautiful. Her marriage was at fifteen.

"In the later years, she moved in with Aunt Sara. They never got along because Sara had a tendency to be sharp. When I was sixteen, I would go stay with them. Grandma would stay in her own room and I'd stay with Aunt Sara. In the morning she would take the yardstick and poke me. She wanted me to come into the kitchen at seven a.m. and have Coffee Royale. She didn't want Sara to know so she wouldn't get any hassle.

"My mother (Mary) didn't approve of Grandma. I can remember sitting at the dining room table and Grandma would have a bottle of Utica Club. She'd swig out of the bottle and Mother would get mad. 'Mama, can't you use a glass?' she'd say. Grandma insisted, 'No, it tastes better out of the bottle.'"

In 1979, Great-Aunt Bessy, at 83 years old and still living at the family homestead in Rome, New York, recalled her mama, Aqualina. "Oh . . . Mama used to dress like you wouldn't believe. There were no flies on Mama. When she lived here, she was the boss of the block. That is when we owned the grocery store and meat market, right over there across the street. The whole family lived right here, 101 Palmer Avenue. Over there in the parking lot is where Papa built his first bread ovens, in the early days. This china chest here, it was Mama's when she was young. Columbus come on Monday and the chest come on Tuesday. That's how old it is."

Aqualina's husband, Thomas Ferlo, the sisters' beloved papa, made it his business

*My grandmother,
Mary Ferlo Scala,
19 years old.*

to help feed the laborers building the Erie Canal. The bakery he founded, eventually taken over by one of my great-uncles, Johnny, floods back into my picture memory at the mere whiff of yeasted dough. As a little girl, my visits to the bakery with Uncle Johnny and his wife Dorothy were the equivalent of being wrapped in a warm blanket.

Great-Aunt Sara remembered her papa's family to me, in 1980. "Papa's parents were from Rogliano, Italy, in the province of Cosenza. Giovanni and Sarafina were their names. I knew Grandpa Ferlo but Sarafina I never knew. She had blonde hair and blue eyes and, according to Mama, a beautiful singing voice.

"They had a home on an olive plantation. Grandpa was the overseer for a count named Bardagio. He also had a mill on the property, you know, and people used to bring their grain to be ground. They had what you used to call a gristmill, where they could grind the grains the old-fashioned way. So that is how my family got into the bread-making business.

"Papa came from Italy to America when he was eight years old with his uncle, the cabinetmaker, just to see it. He worked as a lather boy for a barber in New York City. At sixteen he returned home to Italy and persuaded his family to come to America with him. They came and settled in Utica, New York. He went to school, worked again as a cabinetmaker and then in 1892 moved to Rome, New York. The same year he returned to the old country and married Mama. When he came back, he bought the Wiseborough house where he had the restaurant and saloon. Two years later, he bought the building on South James Street, the building the train ran into in the big wreck. Finally we moved to Palmer Avenue where Bessy still lives today."

All of the sisters, my great-aunts, lovingly shared their memories with me, of each other, their parents and brothers, Joseph, Thomas, Virgilio and John. The social rituals of cooking and feeding people surround every memory and encounter. The Ferlo women lived their everyday lives as a reflection of their Italian culture and heritage. This legacy was beautifully recalled by Valentine about her sister Jane. "I have always called her house the door of hope because she wants everyone to come to her house and once you get there, she smothers you with love and food and comfort. No matter how old you are, even when I go there, she tells me to get into the tub so she can scrub my back."

I couldn't imagine a more important hand-me-down, notable for the effect one might have on another by simply welcoming folks into your home, around the table to share a meal with love to comfort the soul. My recollection of the extended family reunion picnics with all the old-timers is a scene straight out of an Italian movie. Just on the verge of my own womanhood, the five sisters from Rome, New York, sent me on the path I walk today.

My mom and dad, Rosemary and George Scala, created the fertile ground in our own childhood home. I just didn't realize it at the time. They kept our traditions alive,

The sisters and sisters-in-law gather with their mama for a wedding shower.

nurtured them into the present day, updating and evolving with the times, yet remaining true to the core practices established through the lives of our tenacious immigrant forebearers. I credit my non-Italian mother, beautiful Rose, for consistently cooking and adapting many recipes throughout the years until they became standard repertoire for my brothers and me. Now, the next generation is already learning to peel the roasted peppers and cook a decent dish of pasta.

My own children would live on Bruschetta Pomodoro if I let them. While gnocchi in any form is my own family's comfort food, my mom nursed me and my brothers back from every sickness with Stracciatella. She called it rag soup. It's no wonder my curiosity eventually lead me back repeatedly to Italy.

A Neapolitan farmer once told me of a make-ahead fresh tomato sauce, a particular favorite of mine. He puts it up before dawn to "cook" before heading out to the fields; the garlic and olive oil, tomatoes and basil all meld together. Just before meal-

Great-great-grandparents Archangela and Guiseppe Spadaforé.

A newspaper clipping of my grandmother (front center) along with her sisters, parents and grandmother after "the big train wreck." South James Street, Rome, New York.

time, he cooks the pasta and tosses it directly into the sauce.

Whether visiting the Amalfi coast on Italy's western shore of Campania, on the Mediterranean side, or dining in a small fishing village like Grado on the Adriatic Sea, one could dine on tiny local clams the size of a quarter tossed with linguine and served alongside a crisp chilled vino bianco. My mouth waters as I write this just thinking of the Italian technique of cooking vegetables *agrodolce*, which yields a sweet yet tart flavor. Once, while driving through the winding roads of the Ligurian mountains, lost, not a soul in sight, out of nowhere we happened upon a local gathering in celebration of the mushroom; a fungi festival. Everyone was drinking wine and eating sautéed local mushrooms over polenta.

On a cool fall evening in Milan, many years after the meatball argument I first heard upon my grandmother's knee, I discovered the same little nuggets of polpetinni swimming in a rich golden broth of Wedding Soup. Finally, everything came full circle one day in a little *locanda* outside the town of Lucca in Tuscany. Noticing that I was refraining from drinking wine, the proprietress, a beautiful old lady, sat at our table, carefully peeling a succulent peach. She then sliced it into my glass and doused it with sugar and red wine. Without an explanation and wearing the warmest smile ever, she handed it to me and said, "Bueno fortuna," knowing intuitively that I was pregnant. She reminded me of Aunt Jane and the five sisters from Rome, New York, smothering me with love and food and comfort. I hope you use these recipes, gather your family and friends around the dinner table and do the same. ▪

NOTES TO THE COOK

I like to say that when it comes to cooking, simple isn't all that easy. Simple, done well, relies heavily on the understanding of just a couple basic things: good techniques and ingredients. Here is my brief personal list of quirky practices I've picked up over the years to assist my everyday cooking and improve on time, flavor, economy or all three.

BOILING WATER FOR PASTA—The best-cooked noodles will be achieved if you begin with a large pot filled with water—the more the better. The pasta will cook more evenly and be less likely to stick together and be gummy. Once the water is boiled, just before dropping the pasta, add a generous amount of salt until the water tastes "salty like the sea." After you drop the pasta in the boiling, salted water, cover it immediately to hasten the return of the water to a boil, then remove the top and proceed as directed.

CAST IRON—You can't beat a well-seasoned cast-iron skillet for multi-purpose cooking. I have three sizes: fourteen-inch, ten-inch and five-inch. They work as well as any nonstick pan to prevent sticking. Few pans can achieve such a high level of heat on a home stovetop, which is essential for a proper sear. I even bake in them. Besides, at an average price of fifteen dollars, these pans are a bargain and could be handed down through many generations. To season: fill with vegetable oil and place in a 200°F oven for one hour. Cool, discard the oil and wipe out with paper towel. To clean: never use soap. Use salt to rub off any remaining stubborn bits or partially fill with water, bring to a boil on the stovetop and scrape the bottom with a spatula. Pour out the water, return to the stovetop and heat until all the water is evaporated.

FLOURING FOOD FOR SAUTÉING—I have learned from a couple of the finest chefs to keep a container of Wondra gravy flour in the cupboard. Use it when the recipe directs to "dredge" a fillet in flour. This serves to both brown a sautéed food and also to lightly thicken a pan sauce. Wondra is a very light and fine flour, which prevents over-coating and gumminess.

KNIVES—The importance of a decent knife can't be overstated. Invest in a few good knives and keep them sharp. Your cooking experience will be easier, more accurate and safer.

MEAT THERMOMETER—The job of testing doneness of meats is so much easier with a meat thermometer. I'm surprised how many home cooks don't have an instant-read thermometer in the kitchen. Make the investment and not only will it prevent you from prematurely cutting into the meat too soon and losing precious juices, the repeated use will also help you hone your intuitive "doneness" skills.

PARCHMENT PAPER—I keep a role of parchment paper in the kitchen drawer at all times. Use it to line baking sheets; cover a work surface when working with raw meats or as a cooking envelope for steaming food.

ROOM TEMPERATURE MEATS—It is always better and easier to control the cooking of meat if you start with it at room temperature. Try to remember to remove meats from the refrigerator at least thirty minutes before cooking.

SELECTING FRESH INGREDIENTS—Not everyone has the resources or inclination to buy naturally raised or organic foods. I think the more important thing is to buy the freshest, most natural food—closest to its source—whenever possible. But, if you are to invest in one or two organic ingredients, make them chicken and eggs; there is no comparison in flavor or texture to the conventional choice.

WELL-WASHED GREENS—Few things are more frustrating than digging into lovingly made salad or sautéed spinach and chewing on sand. Whether it is lettuce, spinach or kale, I always employ the same method for cleaning. Fill a large bowl or clean sink with cold water. Trim the ends and pick off any bruised or tough leaves. "Float" the greens in the cold water, swishing them around. Let them sit for a couple minutes. Lift the greens out into a colander. Discard the water but notice the cleanliness of the water. Repeat until the water is clean and sand free. I generally give greens three water baths. Spin dry or place the greens side by side on a clean cloth towel in one layer. Cover with paper towel and repeat the layers until finished. Roll up and store the bundle in an opened plastic bag and refrigerate until needed. Also, if a recipe calls for shredded or chopped greens, you can do the chopping before the cleaning process.

INGREDIENTS USED OVER AND OVER IN THIS BOOK

BREADCRUMBS—There are several kinds of breadcrumbs. For the purposes of the rustic cooking in this book, breadcrumbs are easily homemade by accumulating the heels of bread over a week. Process them in a blender or food processor, place in a bag and freeze until needed. Or, if you don't buy whole loaves of bread, it is still best to make your own breadcrumbs from sliced bread. They will have a better flavor and texture than the packaged type you find in most supermarkets.

CANNED TOMATOES—Many recipes in this book call for canned tomatoes. Amongst the brands, the range of taste, acidity and quality is far ranging. I used to only buy imported Italian San Marzano tomatoes. Some brands are excellent but not all. An organic American brand, Muir Glen, consistently delivers the best taste and quality. I always like to buy the tomatoes whole and process them myself to the desired consistency: pureed, chopped, etc.

CAPERS—I learned from many Italian cooks the value of salted capers over brined. If you take the time to properly remove the salt, what is unveiled is a much truer and subtler caper flavor. I recommend floating salted capers in cold water before using, to reduce the saltiness. You can float, drain and repeat until the saltiness is almost completely gone.

EXTRA-VIRGIN OLIVE OIL—Always taste your oil before using it in your food, especially if you don't cook often. Rancid olive oil tastes awful and will ruin your dish. I use extra-virgin olive oil for all of my cooking. If you do tend to use it often, I suggest buying it in quantity, such as a three-liter can, and keeping a small bottle filled on the countertop for immediate use. Store the can in a cool dark place and refill the bottle as needed. Many markets sell a house brand of private label extra-virgin olive oil, which is usually a great value and the freshest choice. Furthermore, I like to keep an additional bottle of very fine, premium extra-virgin olive oil in the pantry, to use with fresh and uncooked dishes to vary the olive oil flavors in a meal. Refrigerate if usage is infrequent.

FRESH HERBS—Parsley and basil are most often called for. Both herbs are very easy to grow on the windowsill or in the garden. If purchasing from the market, wash and store parsley as directed for greens on page 17. Basil is best stored upright in a glass at room temperature, with the roots covered in water, until ready to use.

GARLIC—Most people just buy and use any old garlic. It is such a key player in Italian food that it is worth it to carefully choose firm plump heads with tightly snug cloves. The garlic should not be dried out, shriveled or light in weight for its size. The better the garlic, the more oily the cloves. This amazing allium has a vast range of flavors. You can control the strength and type of flavor in a dish by how you prepare the garlic, i.e., mincing, slicing or crushing the cloves. The end taste also varies tremendously depending on whether garlic is used raw, cooked slightly to unleash its scent, browned or roasted.

PARMESAN AND ROMANO CHEESES—Buy fresh pieces of cheese if possible. Unless you know when your cheese was grated, buying grated cheese is buying less flavor. I keep a small plastic container in the refrigerator filled with wedges of cheese and a handheld grater, and I grate cheese as needed for cooking. At the dinner table, I place a piece of cheese, a cheese knife and the grater on a small plate for guests to help themselves as desired. Along with freshly ground pepper, this is always the "icing on the cake" of your dish.

PASTA—There are many excellent varieties of imported Italian dry pasta available now in the supermarket. Experiment with them to educate yourself because there is a difference in flavor and texture. I always check the package instructions for cooking time, then set my timer for two minutes less and start tasting to assure the perfect doneness. It should be tender yet still slightly firm. This will always make your pasta dishes better if the pasta still has some "tooth" to it rather than being too soft or mushy.

PEPPER, BLACK—Don't underestimate the importance of black pepper, the workhorse of the kitchen. Always keep whole black peppercorns on hand. Grind and keep some in a small dish for quick use and always have a filled pepper mill available for a last-minute grind of fresh pepper. It is worthwhile to invest in a decent pepper mill.

PEPPER, DRIED RED—When used properly, dried red pepper flakes add great dimension to your dishes. If ever a friend travels to Italy, ask them to bring you back some of the small dry red peperoncini. You will taste the heat of the sun. But, the red pepper flakes commercially available will work just fine. Remember, they vary in heat and flavor depending on their age and exposure to air so taste before using.

SALT—I recommend a coarse kosher salt for everyday cooking. I love to have a couple specialty salts in the cupboard to add further dimension to the finish of some dishes.

DRINKS AND APPETIZERS

ARANCIATA COCKTAIL

MAKES 3 SERVINGS

I developed this cocktail out of love for San Pellegrino's outstanding sparkling natural orange beverage, Aranciata, which is an essential ingredient for this mix—substitutes simply don't taste the same. One must also have a bottle of angostura bitters on hand which is a liquid mixture of aromatic herbs, roots and plants, often called for to flavor drinks. This drink became an instant hit in my house and my husband named it the "Cindacious," now affectionately referred to only as a "Dacious."

1 lime, cut in 6 wedges
Several dashes angostura aromatic bitters
4½ ounces golden rum, such as Appleton
1 (11.5-ounce) can San Pellegrino Aranciata orange soda

■ Fill three 12-ounce glasses to the top with ice. Squeeze a wedge of lime over the ice in each glass, leaving the squeezed rind in the glass. Shake a generous dash of bitters over the ice. Pour 1½ ounces of rum into each glass. Fill each glass to the top with the Aranciata and stir vigorously. Garnish with an additional wedge of lime and serve.

FRUIT AND FRESH HERB CARAFE

MAKES 6 SERVINGS

One day while dining at one of my favorite Tuscan restaurants, I mentioned to the chef, Cesare Casella, that I'd remembered having a drink in Italy where fruit was crushed with herbs to which liquor and Prosecco sparkling wine was added. He wasted no time going behind the bar to make a batch, saying that he'd always had such a drink which he called "Carafe" on the menu of his family's restaurant, Vipore, in Lucca, Italy. This is my version of what Cesare made for me that day. Choose the freshest, ripest available fruit.

4 cups fresh fruit, such as sliced peaches or strawberries
3 tablespoons sugar
5 sprigs fresh basil, plus more for garnish
¾ cup vodka
1 bottle Italian sparkling wine such as Prosecco or Lambrusco, chilled

In a large pitcher, place the fruit, sugar and basil. Using a wooden spoon, crush the mixture until it forms a rough mash. Stir in the vodka. Just before serving, pour the Prosecco over the mixture and serve immediately over ice. Garnish with a sprig of fresh basil.

HANDMADE CAPPUCCINO

MAKES 1 LARGE MUG

This is how I have my coffee every morning. While I've used excellent home espresso machines, nothing is better to me than this handmade method. All it requires is a stovetop espresso pot, which is available at most housewares stores for under twenty dollars. I've also tried dozens of coffees and find Illy brand espresso, fine grind, to be the tastiest for this method. I haven't figured out why, but some milk foams better than others and it doesn't depend on fat content so don't give up if you don't get a good foam—just try a different brand.

8 ounces water
¼ cup espresso ground coffee (preferably Illy espresso coffee, fine grind)
8 ounces milk
Sugar (optional)

■ Pour the water into the bottom chamber of the stovetop espresso pot. Fill the filter basket which fits over the water with the coffee, tamping down gently. Place on the stovetop burner over medium-low heat. Watch carefully and remove from the heat as soon as the intense boiling has stopped, about 2 minutes. It is complete when all the water has boiled through the filter into the top part of the pot.

■ Meanwhile, place the milk in a 16-ounce coffee mug. Heat in the microwave until hot but not starting to bubble on the sides. (Alternatively, you may heat the milk on the stovetop in a small pan, then transfer to a mug.)

■ Hold the handle of a small 4-inch whisk between the palms of both hands. Put the whisk in the hot milk and twirl rapidly back and forth until foam appears on the top, about 20 seconds. Pour the coffee into the mug. Sweeten if desired and serve immediately.

ROASTED PEPPERS

MAKES 6 TO 8 SERVINGS

This is one of the recipes that all three of my brothers and our dad make often, although I think we all make them slightly differently. The next generation of family cooks is already in training, assisting in the peeling, cleaning and eating. Most often these versatile peppers are served before the meal with cheese and sopressata salami. Try serving them as a side dish for roasted meats, mixed with sautéed potatoes or used in any egg dish, be it frittata, scrambled or tucked under the yolk of a one-eye egg on toast. Choose peppers without blemishes or wrinkled skin, as they will be fresher and therefore much easier to peel.

4 fresh red bell peppers, can use yellow or orange instead or a combination
¼ cup extra-virgin olive oil
4 cloves garlic, peeled and thinly sliced
2 teaspoons coarse salt

▪ If using a gas stove, turn the stovetop burner flame to medium-high. Place a pepper directly into the flame and heat until charred and black on all sides, turning with tongs to complete. Immediately place the pepper into a paper or plastic bag and allow to sit for 15 to 20 minutes, and repeat with the remaining peppers. Alternatively, slice peppers in half lengthwise, remove the seeds and core and lay cut side down on a rimmed baking sheet. Place under a preheated broiler and watch carefully until the skin is charred, rotating the baking sheet if necessary for even cooking. Remove from the oven, cover peppers with foil on the pan, let sit for 15 to 20 minutes, and proceed as directed.

▪ Scrape off the charred skin from the peppers; it should come off easily. Slice the peppers lengthwise into ½-inch strips. (I believe my brothers stop here and simply combine the pepper strips with the oil, garlic, salt and serve. You may too.)

▪ Heat the olive oil and garlic in a large skillet over medium heat until it begins to bubble but not brown, about 30 seconds. Add the peppers and salt; reduce the heat to low and cover. Cook gently until the peppers reach the desired tenderness, 5 to 8 minutes. Taste for salt. Serve as desired (see Headnote). The peppers will keep, covered, in the refrigerator for up to 1 week.

BRUSCHETTA POMODORO

MAKES 6 APPETIZER SERVINGS (20 PIECES)

This is the favorite snack of my third-born boy, Luca. When the whole extended family gathers together to prepare a meal, the children pitch in to help make the tomato topping, which can be prepared without a knife by simply ripping the tomatoes and basil by hand into the bowl. The adults and children eat every last bit up before supper. Use the freshest and best possible tomatoes. The tomato mixture can also be tossed with cooked pasta for a fresh sauce.

One 8-inch loaf round Italian bread, cut in half crosswise, and cut into 10 slices per side
3 tablespoons extra-virgin olive oil
4 to 6 Roma tomatoes, cut into 1-inch dice (about 3 cups)
⅓ cup fresh basil leaves, cleaned, stacked in a pile, rolled and cut into a fine julienne
6 cloves garlic, 3 crushed and 3 cut in half lengthwise
2 teaspoons coarse salt
Freshly ground black pepper

■ Preheat the oven to 450°F. Set the oven rack in the top part of the oven.

■ Place sliced bread on rimmed baking sheets. Cook 10 minutes or until lightly toasted. Flip bread and toast 5 more minutes.

■ Meanwhile, in a medium-size bowl, place the olive oil, tomatoes, basil, 3 crushed garlic cloves, salt and pepper. Stir to combine.

■ Rub the 3 halved garlic cloves, cut side down, over every piece of toasted bread. Spoon a couple tablespoons of tomato mixture over each piece of toast and serve immediately.

MINIATURE MEATBALL PANINI

MAKES 8 TO 10 APPETIZER SERVINGS (56 PIECES)

My non-Italian mom made these for us every Christmas, so I think of them as Rose's sandwiches. She served them as appetizers and we used to eat them like peanuts. When I referred to them as Rose's Mini Meatball Sandwiches on television, my Italian father phoned to say, rather indignantly, "Those are your grandmother's sandwiches." But, it was mom who made them a family staple for our generation. Bake the cut-off crusts separately for a delicious chef's treat. You can prepare, bake, cool, freeze and then store them in an airtight plastic bag. Just thaw and reheat at 325°F for 12 minutes.

1 loaf thin-sliced white bread, such as Pepperidge Farm
2 teaspoons extra-virgin olive oil
1 pound ground pork, or a combination beef and pork
1 large egg
¼ cup freshly grated Romano cheese
¼ cup freshly grated Parmesan cheese
¼ cup finely chopped fresh flat-leaf parsley
1 clove garlic
½ teaspoon dried oregano
½ teaspoon dried thyme
¼ teaspoon coarse salt
Freshly ground black pepper
8 tablespoons (1 stick) unsalted butter, softened to room temperature

■ Preheat the oven to 350°F.

■ In a food processor or blender, process the ends of the loaf of bread to fine breadcrumbs, about ½ cup. Set the remaining bread aside.

■ In a large bowl, combine the olive oil, meat, egg, cheeses, parsley, garlic, oregano, thyme, salt, pepper and breadcrumbs. Mix with your hands to combine well.

■ Roll the meat mixture into 1-inch balls and reserve on a baking sheet. Lay 2 slices of bread on work surface. Butter one side of each piece. Place 4 meatballs on the buttered surface of the slice of bread. Top with a second slice of bread, buttered side down, and press firmly to adhere. Use a serrated knife to cut the crusts from the bread. Bake the crusts separately for a "chef's treat." Cut the sandwich into 4 equal squares. Transfer to a parchment-lined, rimmed baking sheet. Repeat with the remaining meatballs and bread. This process can be done assembly-line style, lining up slices of buttered bread and assembling a number at a time. Prepare 2 baking sheets at a time if possible.

■ Bake for 15 to 20 minutes or until golden brown. Repeat, if necessary, until all sandwiches are cooked. Remove from the pan and cool. Serve slightly warm.

TUNA GREMOLATA DIP

MAKES 6 TO 8 SERVINGS

I was pleasantly surprised to find this in my grandmother's recipe file. Oddly, she called it Gremolata and noted it as a "vegetable dip." Until then, I'd only seen the word gremolata used to reference a garnish of parsley, lemon and garlic tradition-ally used with Osso Buco (page 99). But, like so many things, who knows how this word became Nonny's title for a tuna dip? It's like a smooth tuna salad but without mayonnaise and with quintessential Italian flavorings. Use your favorite canned tuna or splurge on the imported olive oil–packed tuna from Sicily, which is avail-able in specialty food shops. The dip keeps well for a few days refrigerated. Nonny suggested serving this with fresh celery, radishes and carrots but I also like to offer thin, crispy crackers.

1 (7-ounce) can tuna, preferably packed
  in olive oil, drained
2 tablespoons extra-virgin olive oil
3 tablespoons fresh lemon juice (about
  2 small lemons)
¾ cup chopped onion
¾ cup chopped fresh flat-leaf parsley
1 teaspoon minced garlic
1 tablespoon capers, washed and drained
½ teaspoon coarse salt
⅛ teaspoon freshly ground black pepper
Fresh-cut vegetables, or crackers, for
  serving

■ Place the tuna in a blender or food processor and pulse to break it up. Turn on low speed and add the olive oil, lemon juice, onion, parsley, garlic, capers, salt and pepper, one at a time, until they are thoroughly combined and the mixture is smooth. Place in a small bowl and serve with fresh-cut vegetables or crackers on the side.

PANCETTA FRITTATA

MAKES 4 MEAL SERVINGS, OR 8 TO 10 APPETIZER SERVINGS

A frittata is an Italian-style omelet—started on the stovetop and finished in the oven. Serve it for brunch with an arugula salad or as a light supper. If cut in 1½-inch squares it makes a perfect appetizer. If you have it—a well-seasoned cast-iron skillet is the perfect choice for the transfer from stove-top to oven to table.

6 slices pancetta (about 2 ounces), thinly sliced
6 large eggs
2 tablespoons water
½ pound fresh mozzarella, cut into ¼-inch slices
1 tablespoon chopped fresh flat-leaf parsley
1 tablespoon shredded fresh basil leaves
Freshly ground black pepper

■ Preheat the broiler.

■ Place the pancetta in a 10-inch cast-iron pan or oven-proof nonstick skillet over high heat. Fry until crisp, about 2 minutes per side. Pour off any excess fat. Meanwhile, beat the eggs and water together until foamy. Position the meat evenly around the pan and pour the egg mixture over the pancetta. Reduce the heat to medium and cook for 1 to 2 minutes, swirling the eggs around the pan as it begins to cook.

■ Transfer the pan to the broiler and cook until the eggs begin to set, about 2 minutes longer. Place the cheese slices around the frittata and return to the broiler. Broil until cheese is melted and bubbly, from 30 seconds to 1 minute. Remove from the oven and sprinkle with parsley, basil and pepper. Cut as desired and serve immediately.

PROSCIUTTO WITH FRESH FRUIT

MAKES 8 SERVINGS

This classic combination of salty prosciutto with sweet cool melon is a refreshing way to start any meal. I like to use different kinds of fruits depending on what is the freshest available offering. Using a selection of different colored and textured melons is also very beautiful. For bite-sized hors d'oeuvres, cut the fruit into small pieces, wrap each piece with prosciutto, cut to size and serve with toothpicks.

1 medium-size ripe melon, peeled and cut into 8 wedges, 8 figs or 8 halved peaches
2 limes or lemons, 1 cut in half, 1 cut in 8 wedges for garnish
Freshly ground black pepper (optional)
1 pound prosciutto, best quality, thinly sliced

■ Cut the fruit into the desired size. Squeeze the halved citrus over all the fruit. Crack freshly ground pepper over it, if desired. Place a piece on each plate and lay the prosciutto over each piece of fruit, cutting to size if necessary. Serve a wedge of citrus on the side.

GRILLED CALAMARI

MAKES 4 APPETIZER SERVINGS

Calamari is one of the simplest things to cook as long as you follow this adage: cook really fast or really slow. Anything in between and the texture is too chewy.
Get your fishmonger to clean the calamari and then all you have to do is wash, dry and slice it. Serve this in a big bowl as a part of an antipasti spread or on its own in small serving bowls.

¼ cup extra-virgin olive oil
1½ tablespoons fresh lemon juice (1 small lemon)
½ teaspoon coarse salt
1 clove garlic, thinly sliced
2 sprigs fresh oregano, or ½ teaspoon dried
1 pound fresh squid, cleaned, rinsed and well dried
Freshly ground black pepper

■ In a serving bowl, whisk together the olive oil, lemon juice and salt. Stir in the garlic and whole oregano sprigs.

■ Heat a grill pan over high heat. (Alternatively, you can cook the squid on the grill.) When very hot, add the squid and char each side for 1 minute. Remove from the pan and slice crosswise into ¼-inch rings, including the tendrils. Add the squid to the lemon sauce. Crack freshly ground pepper over and serve immediately.

PASTA

SPAGHETTI POMODORO

MAKES 4 TO 6 SERVINGS

This is the most basic, standby meal in our household since everything is in the pantry. Growing up we had versions of sauce that cooked for hours or contained onions and other herbs. After experimenting, I settled on my own pared-down recipe in Italy years ago when we were staying in a little farmhouse on top of the hill in Pedona di Camaiore in Tuscany. When not cooking ourselves, we'd walk over to the only little restaurant in town called Il Soggiorno carrying our pasta serving bowl. There, they'd fill our bowl with the evening's special pasta and we'd head back home to eat so our then two-year-old firstborn boy, Calder, could sleep. The secret to their sauce is using just a few of the best ingredients cooked briefly. I use this sauce for lasagna, baked ziti or anytime a basic red sauce is required.

2 tablespoons extra-virgin olive oil, plus more for drizzling
2 cloves garlic, finely minced
Pinch red pepper flakes
1 (28-ounce) can best-quality whole tomatoes, lightly pulsed in a blender
½ teaspoon salt
Freshly ground black pepper
Small pinch sugar
1 sprig fresh basil
1 pound spaghetti
Freshly grated Parmesan cheese

■ Bring a large pot of water to boil.

■ Place the olive oil and garlic in a 2-quart saucepan over medium heat. Swirl the pan to coat the garlic with oil and heat until garlic sizzles but doesn't brown, about 30 seconds. Add the red pepper flakes and stir. Add the tomatoes, salt, black pepper and sugar and stir to combine. Bring to a boil and reduce the heat to a simmer. Cook for at least 20 minutes but no more than 30. Add the basil for last 5 minutes of cooking. Remove the basil before serving.

■ Meanwhile, with 10 minutes to spare before the sauce is done, generously salt the boiling water. Add the pasta and cook until tender but slightly firm. Set the timer for 2 minutes less than the package instructions specify and taste for doneness. Drain the pasta and transfer it to a serving bowl. Toss with ½ cup of the sauce. For each serving, spoon on a little extra sauce, grated Parmesan cheese, a drizzle of olive oil and freshly ground pepper on top of the pasta.

FETTUCCINE ALLA CARBONARA

MAKES 4 TO 6 SERVINGS

This is the hands-down favorite pasta dish of my second-born boy, Miles, our only picky eater who, if asked his choice for dinner, chooses Carbonara. Needless to say, the others have also had more than their share of this "bacon and eggs" sauce. It is a classic Roman preparation, authentically prepared without cream, which I prefer, although many recipes call for it.

2 tablespoons extra-virgin olive oil
2 cloves garlic, smashed and peeled
1 pound pancetta or mildly smoked bacon,
   cut crosswise into thin strips
Dash white wine, or red would be fine too
2 large eggs
½ cup freshly grated Parmesan cheese,
   plus more for serving
2 tablespoons finely chopped parsley
Freshly ground black pepper
1 pound fettuccine pasta, or substitute
   spaghetti

■ Bring a large pot of water to a boil.

■ Place the olive oil and garlic in a large skillet over medium heat, tilting the pan to cover the cloves in oil, and allow the cloves to sizzle until slightly golden, about 1½ minutes. Remove the garlic and add the pancetta. Cook, stirring occasionally until the fat is completely rendered and the pancetta is slightly crisp, about 6 minutes. Drain off most of the fat, increase the heat to high and add the wine. Cook for about 30 seconds or until the wine evaporates. Set aside.

■ Meanwhile, in a large serving bowl, whisk the eggs and stir in the cheese, parsley and pepper.

■ Meanwhile, generously salt the boiling water. Add the pasta and cook until tender but slightly firm. Set the timer for 2 minutes less than the package instructions specify and taste for doneness. Drain the pasta and immediately add it to the egg mixture while still very hot. Toss the pasta to coat completely with the egg mixture. Add the bacon and toss to distribute evenly. Serve with Parmesan cheese and freshly ground pepper.

GNOCCHI WITH PESTO

MAKES 6 SERVINGS

Homemade gnocchi is very simple and much easier than pasta to make once you get the hang of it. It's also one of the first cooking projects I involved the kids in. These little potato dumplings are light as clouds. The trick is to completely cool your potatoes before kneading in the remaining ingredients. Instead of Pesto, you can also serve it with butter and cheese, Pomodoro sauce (page 41) or Ragu (page 51). They can be made a couple hours ahead and kept covered with a towel until ready to cook and serve.

3 best-quality Idaho potatoes, washed and dried
2 cups all-purpose flour
1 tablespoon coarse salt
1 recipe Pesto (see page 46)

■ Preheat the oven to 350°F.

■ Spear the potatoes lightly with a fork in a few paces. Place directly on the oven rack and cook until completely tender, about 1 hour. When cool enough to handle, cut the potatoes open, scoop out the flesh, and pass it through a potato ricer to achieve a very fine and light texture. Spread out on a rimmed baking sheet and allow to cool completely (very important).

■ In a mixing bowl, whisk together 1¾ cups of the flour and the salt. Slowly blend the flour mixture into the potatoes, using your hands to combine completely, until the dough pulls away from your hands and feels like pizza dough. Add flour if necessary to achieve desired consistency.

■ Sprinkle some flour on a clean work surface. Separate the dough into several pieces and roll out each into the size of a cigar. Cut each "cigar" into 1-inch pieces. To form the gnocchi, dip a fork in flour, then place the tines on top of a piece of dough. Applying medium pressure, gently roll the gnocchi toward you with the fork, releasing pressure gradually as you roll, until it is completely rolled off the tines. Repeat with each piece of dough, placing the gnocchi on a floured baking sheet as completed. The pieces should resemble tiny footballs with a cup in the center.

■ Place a large pot of water on the stove to boil. When boiling, add a generous amount of salt. Drop about 8 gnocchi into the water at a time and cook until they return to float on the surface of the boiling water, 2 to 3 minutes. Remove with a slotted spoon and toss immediately with the Pesto.

PESTO

MAKES ⅔ CUP

Pesto is a very familiar and well-known fresh basil sauce, which originates in the Ligurian region of Italy. I love it with gnocchi but Nonny's family recipe recommends serving it with spaghetti. Her recipe excluded Parmesan, which is still good, but it's better, I think, with the cheese. It freezes well so you can make a big batch when the basil is fresh and beautiful. Or, it can stay in the fridge in a jar for a couple of days with olive oil poured on top to prevent darkening.

**2 cups fresh basil leaves, without
blemishes, cleaned and dried
2 cloves garlic, minced
¼ cup pine nuts
¼ cup freshly grated Parmesan cheese
1 teaspoon salt
Freshly ground black pepper
⅓ cup extra-virgin olive oil**

■ Place the basil, garlic, pine nuts, cheese, salt and pepper in a blender or food processor. Blend for 10 seconds. With the machine running, gradually pour in the olive oil until the mixture is smooth.

FUSILLI WITH BROCCOLI

This is another standard dish in our home, easily made in the time it takes to cook the pasta. Perfect for teaching kids to eat their vegetables but always devoured by the adults too. I serve it as a quick supper, sometimes with a dollop of ricotta cheese on the side, or as a starter for a large meal which includes roast pork.

1 pound fusilli pasta, or other short macaroni like ziti or penne
1 head broccoli, florets removed, stem peeled and sliced into coins
¼ cup extra-virgin olive oil, plus more for serving
2 cloves garlic, minced
Pinch red pepper flakes
¼ cup freshly grated Parmesan cheese, plus more for serving
Freshly ground black pepper
1 cup ricotta cheese (optional)

■ Bring a large pot of water to a boil. Generously salt the boiling water, add the fusilli and boil for 6 minutes. Add the broccoli florets and coins to the boiling pasta and cover until the water comes back to a boil. Boil 4 more minutes. The pasta and broccoli should both be tender. Drain the pasta and broccoli, reserving ⅓ cup of the cooking water.

■ Place the olive oil, garlic and red pepper flakes in a large saucepan and heat over medium heat until the garlic begins to sizzle and turn lightly golden, about 1 minute. Stir the reserved ⅓ cup of pasta cooking water into the pan. Add the pasta and broccoli to the saucepan. Add the Parmesan cheese and toss to combine. Serve with more grated cheese and black pepper on top. Drizzle with olive oil. Scoop a spoonful of ricotta cheese on the side of the pasta, if desired.

BUCATINI PUTTANESCA

MAKES 4 TO 6 SERVINGS

This sauce originated from the Amalfi coast in Italy. I was taught to cook the foods of this region in Positano at the home of Dianna Folinari who had the most friendly and fun cooking school in her apartment overlooking the sea. Puttanesca is derived from the word puttana, meaning "whore," which is said to have been named for its ability to attract eaters with its hot and fiery nature. Even tastier if made a day ahead, Puttanesca sauce also pairs beautifully with fish. Bucatini are the long, thick and hollow spaghetti-like strands, similar to perciatelli.

1½ tablespoons extra-virgin olive oil
2 cloves garlic, minced
½ cup black olives, such as Gaeta or Niçoise, rinsed, pitted and thinly sliced
½ cup green olives Italian-style, rinsed, pitted and coarsely chopped
3 tablespoons capers, preferably salt-packed, thoroughly soaked and rinsed
½ teaspoon red pepper flakes, plus more for serving
1 (28-ounce) can best-quality tomatoes, half pureed, half roughly crushed
1 sprig fresh basil, plus more for garnish
½ teaspoon dried oregano
1 pound bucatini pasta
Freshly grated Parmesan cheese

■ Bring a large pot of water to a boil.

■ Place olive oil and garlic in a large saucepan. Heat over medium heat until the garlic begins to sizzle but not brown, about 30 seconds. Add the olives, capers and ¼ teaspoon of the red pepper flakes. Add the pureed and crushed tomatoes, bring to a boil, reduce the heat and simmer for 15 minutes. Add the basil sprig, the remaining ¼ teaspoon red pepper flakes and the oregano and cook for an additional 10 minutes.

■ Meanwhile, generously salt the boiling water. Add the pasta and cook until tender but still firm. Set the timer for 2 minutes less than the package instructions specify and taste for doneness. Drain the pasta and toss with the sauce. Serve with additional red pepper flakes, grated Parmesan cheese and freshly torn basil leaves.

RIGATONI WITH RAPID RAGU

MAKES 6 SERVINGS

Although a totally different animal from a typical long-cooking beef ragu, this quick recipe is packed with flavor. It is a great weeknight dinner if you're craving a meat sauce but haven't the time for an authentic slow-cooked version. The secret flavor weapon is mortadella—a slow smoked sausage which originated in Bologna, Italy, made from pork, beef, fat and seasonings. It is available in the deli section of most markets. My husband quite unexpectedly developed this recipe with the leftover mortadella he uses in his signature Polpette (page 101), another recipe beloved by everyone who tastes it.

2 tablespoons extra-virgin olive oil
3 cloves garlic, minced
1½ tablespoons tomato paste
¾ pound ground pork
½ pound mortadella, chopped fine
8 ounces tomato sauce, can use canned if
   you don't have homemade
3 tablespoons fresh flat-leaf parsley
1 pound rigatoni pasta
Freshly grated Parmesan cheese
Freshly ground black pepper

■ Bring a large pot of water to a boil.

■ Put the olive oil and garlic in a heavy-bottomed 2-quart saucepan over medium heat and cook until the garlic sizzles and is slightly golden, about 1 minute. Stir in the tomato paste and cook for 1 minute. Add the pork and mortadella and cook, while stirring, until the pinkness is eliminated, about 10 minutes. Stir in the tomato sauce and 1 tablespoon of water. Reduce the heat to low and cook for 20 minutes, stirring occasionally. Stir in the parsley.

■ Meanwhile, with 15 minutes left for the sauce to cook, generously salt the boiling water. Add the rigatoni and cook until tender but still firm. Set the timer for 2 minutes less than the package instructions specify and taste for doneness. Toss the rigatoni with the sauce and serve topped with Parmesan cheese and pepper.

MOSTACCIOLI AMATRACIANA

MAKES 4 TO 6 SERVINGS

Next to Linguine with Clams (page 55), this is my favorite pasta dish. I will always order it if it is on the menu when I'm in an Italian restaurant, and like so many dishes, the preparation really varies. I've had it slightly creamy, with chopped hard-boiled egg on top and over many different types of pasta. You may substitute your favorite noodle too.

2 tablespoons extra-virgin olive oil
4 ounces thick-cut pancetta or lightly smoked bacon, cut in ¼-inch cubes
2 tablespoons unsalted butter
4 shallots, peeled and sliced crosswise (about ¼ cup)
½ teaspoon red pepper flakes
1 (28-ounce) can whole tomatoes, with juices, lightly pulsed in food processor or blender
1 pound mostaccioli, or bucatini is good too
Freshly grated Pecorino Romano cheese, or can also use Parmesan

▧ Bring a large pot of water to boil.

▧ Place 1 tablespoon of the olive oil and the pancetta in a large skillet over high heat and cook until the fat is completely rendered and the pancetta is crispy, about 6 to 8 minutes. Pour off the fat and reduce the heat to medium-low. Add the remaining tablespoon of olive oil and 1 tablespoon of the butter. Add the shallots and red pepper flakes and cook, stirring, for 1 minute. Add the tomatoes and bring to a boil. Reduce the heat and simmer, stirring occasionally, for 30 minutes. Swirl in the remaining tablespoon of butter.

▧ Meanwhile, generously salt the boiling water. Add the mostaccioli and cook until tender but still firm. Set the timer for 2 minutes less than the package instructions specify and taste for doneness. Drain the pasta and add it to the sauce. Toss to coat and serve topped with freshly grated Pecorino Romano cheese.

LINGUINE WITH CLAMS

MAKES 4 TO 6 SERVINGS

This is my favorite pasta dish, so when I can get fresh small clams, I will often make it several days in a row. I tasted my favorite version in Positano, Italy, several years ago and it was a real revelation. It is notable for its omission of white wine, which allows for the subtle clam flavor to shine. I do love to serve it with wine though, a cool crisp bottle of white such as Vermentino or even rosés. If you get an early start, the main flavor technique here is to marinate your garlic in olive oil for as long as possible. It's traditional to drizzle chile-infused oil over this dish just before serving; combine ¼ cup of extra-virgin olive oil and a teaspoon of red pepper flakes in a cruet, let it marinate for several hours and pass it around at the table.

⅓ cup extra-virgin olive oil
4 cloves garlic, 2 smashed and peeled, 2 thinly sliced
¼ teaspoon red pepper flakes
3 dozen littleneck clams or 4 dozen cockles
1 tablespoon cornmeal or flour
1 pound linguine pasta
3 tablespoons chopped fresh flat-leaf parsley

▦ Up to 8 hours in advance but as little as 1, place the olive oil, garlic and red pepper flakes in a large pasta serving bowl. Cover and let stand at room temperature.

▦ To clean the clams, rinse them and place in large bowl with cold water and the cornmeal or flour. The live clams open to ingest the cornmeal, thereby releasing any remaining sand. Let soak 10 minutes. Scrub each clam clean under cold running water to remove remaining, softened mud from the shell and return to soak in fresh cold water. If necessary, repeat the scrubbing process a couple times until the clams are completely clean and soaking water is free of sand. Drain and chill until ready to cook.

▦ Bring a large pot of water to a boil. Generously salt the boiling water, add the linguine and cook until tender but still firm. Set the timer for 2 minutes less than the package instructions specify and taste for doneness.

■ Meanwhile, in a large pot with a tight-fitting lid, bring ¼ cup of water to a boil. Add the cleaned clams, cover immediately and steam until the clams are open, 3 to 5 minutes. Discard any clams that do not open.

■ Place the cooked clams with the shells into the marinated olive oil. Strain the cooked clam liquid into the bowl. Add pasta and parsley and toss. Serve immediately with a drizzle of spicy olive oil on top.

VEGETABLES AND SALADS

BAKED ARTICHOKES

MAKES 6 SERVINGS

Evolved from my grandmother's recipe for whole baked artichokes, my mom invented this version in order to more easily feed a large crowd. It is a staple side dish on our Thanksgiving table. It is the dish we all covet and the first leftover I look for next morning on the off chance it wasn't devoured. To use whole artichokes instead, just clean and trim the artichokes and pack the crumb topping around the leaves. Fit them snugly in a dish, drizzle with dressing and cook using the same method until they are tender. Frozen artichokes are usually sold cut in pieces with a few leaves attached.

1½ cups fresh breadcrumbs
¼ cup finely chopped fresh flat-leaf parsley
¼ cup freshly grated Parmesan cheese
¼ cup freshly grated Romano cheese
1 tablespoon combined dried herbs such as thyme, oregano and savory or herbs sold as Italian Seasoning
½ teaspoon coarse salt
Freshly ground black pepper
⅔ cup extra-virgin olive oil
¼ cup fresh lemon juice
2 cloves garlic, minced
3 (9-ounce) packages best-quality frozen artichoke hearts, thawed and drained

■ Preheat the oven to 325°F.

■ In a medium bowl, mix together the breadcrumbs, parsley, cheeses, dried herbs, salt and pepper. Set aside.

■ In another bowl, whisk together the olive oil, lemon juice and garlic. Set aside.

■ Rub olive oil inside a 13 x 9-inch-size rectangular Pyrex™ baking dish. Lay the artichokes side by side in the baking dish. Evenly distribute the crumb topping over the artichokes, pushing it down in between the hearts. Tap the dish on the counter allowing the crumbs to sink in the cracks.

■ Drizzle the dressing all over the crumb topping. Cover the dish with foil and bake for 30 minutes. Increase the temperature to 375°F, remove the foil and bake an additional 10 to 15 minutes or until the top is golden brown all over.

TUSCAN KALE

I love every kind of kale, and it is such a healthy vegetable to include in your diet. Shredded and cooked over high heat with olive oil, it caramelizes slightly and needs nothing more than a little salt to taste delicious. You may use regular kale for this dish if unable to find Tuscan, which has a long, slender, dark green leaf. It is an excellent side dish to serve with roasted or grilled meats.

3 tablespoons extra-virgin olive oil
2 bunches Tuscan kale or 1 bunch
regular kale, ends trimmed off and cut
crosswise into ¼-inch strips, rinsed well
with water still clinging to the leaves
Coarse salt to taste

■ Heat a large cast-iron skillet over high heat. Add the olive oil and just before it smokes, little by little add the some of the kale to the pan, adding more as each addition begins to collapse. Continue to cook and stir until the water is evaporated and the kale starts to caramelize a little, about 10 minutes. Add salt to taste.

SAUTÉED MUSHROOMS

MAKES 6 SERVINGS WITH POLENTA OR PASTA

Until I learned this technique, I was always careful to wipe off, not wash, mushrooms because I wanted them very dry for a quick sauté in which the outside is brown and the moisture remains inside. Conversely, this recipe directs to wash in water and cover at the outset, drawing out the moisture initially and letting it brown in the final stages. The texture is different and the flavor is very deep. Serve this over polenta or steak or folded into risotto. It also forms the base for an excellent pasta sauce by simply adding a dash of white wine, $\frac{1}{4}$ cup of cream and 3 tablespoons grated cheese.

1½ pounds fresh mushrooms
½ lemon
3 cloves garlic, minced
3 tablespoons extra-virgin olive oil
1½ teaspoons coarse salt
¼ teaspoon freshly ground black pepper
2 tablespoons chopped fresh flat-leaf parsley

■ Submerge the mushrooms in cold water, swish around to wash thoroughly and drain. Trim the ends, slice and place in a large bowl. Squeeze the juice of the lemon half over the mushrooms and toss.

■ Put the garlic in a large pan and pour in the olive oil. Heat over medium-high heat until the garlic begins to sizzle but not brown, about 30 seconds. Add the mushrooms, stir and cover. Cook, stirring occasionally, for 4 minutes.

■ Remove the lid, add the salt and pepper and cook, stirring, until all the moisture is evaporated and the mushrooms begin to brown, about 5 minutes. Stir in the parsley and serve.

CARROTS AGRODOLCE

MAKES 4 TO 6 SERVINGS

This is an outstanding technique for cooking vegetables. Agrodolce means sweet and sour, a taste usually achieved through the use of sugar and vinegar. I like to include these carrots as a part of a vegetable antipasti as they are delicious served at room temperature and therefore can be made ahead of time. I also like to prepare zucchini in this method but I would sauté it in olive oil before proceeding to step two.

1 pound carrots, peeled and sliced into matchsticks, cut carrot in half crosswise, then slice into lengthwise slabs, stack slabs on top of each other and finely slice into matchsticks
1½ tablespoons extra-virgin olive oil
¾ teaspoon coarse salt
2 tablespoons minced onion
¾ teaspoon sugar
1 tablespoon red wine vinegar
¼ teaspoon freshly ground black pepper
2 tablespoons fresh mint (optional)

■ Place the carrots, olive oil, ¼ teaspoon of the salt and ⅓ cup water in a large saucepan over high heat. Bring to a boil and cook until the water has evaporated, about 7 minutes.

■ Stir in the onion and cook for 1 minute. Add the sugar and mix. Add the vinegar, pepper and remaining ½ teaspoon of salt and stir until there is a glaze coating the carrots, about 30 seconds. Remove from the heat and stir in the mint, if desired. Place on serving platter.

GREEN BEANS WITH TOMATO AND BASIL

MAKES 6 SERVINGS

You may use green or yellow beans for this dish. The vegetables are well cooked in a typical Italian style, which happens to work very well with green beans. Usually served as a side dish, I could eat a whole bowl of these with crusty bread and be happy. Serve with Carrots Agrodolce (page 62) as vegetable antipasti.

1 pound green beans, trimmed
2 tablespoons extra-virgin olive oil
1 tomato, cored and chopped
2 cloves garlic, thinly sliced
1 teaspoon coarse salt
¼ teaspoon red pepper flakes
1 large sprig fresh basil

Rinse and drain the beans; there should be water left clinging to the beans. Place the olive oil, tomato, garlic, salt, red pepper flakes and basil in a medium-size saucepan with a tight-fitting lid. Add the wet beans and cover. Cook over medium-low heat, stirring occasionally until the beans are soft and tender, about 15 minutes.

Remove the cover, add the basil sprig and cook until most of the juices are evaporated, about 5 minutes. Remove basil sprig before serving.

SPINACH WITH LEMON

MAKES 4 TO 6 SERVINGS

This side dish is eaten weekly at our dinner table, and leftovers are often folded into the next morning's eggs. I've updated this recipe by eliminating the step of blanching before sautéing in favor of the slightest steaming and dressing. Critical here is the thorough washing of the fresh spinach. First trim the ends and then place it in a large bowl of cold water. Swish it around and let float for a minute. Repeat two or usually three times or until the water is clean. Place in a colander—the water should still be clinging to the leaves for cooking.

2 bunches fresh spinach (about 1¾ pounds), cleaned and still wet (see above)
3 tablespoons extra-virgin olive oil
1 lemon, cut in half crosswise
½ teaspoon coarse salt
Freshly ground black pepper

■ Place the spinach in a large pot with a tight-fitting lid. Cover and cook over high heat, turning leaves halfway through to move the bottom wilted leaves to the top, until the spinach is just barely wilted and tender, about 4 minutes.

■ Lift the spinach into a warm serving dish. Drizzle over the olive oil and the juice from half the lemon. Sprinkle on the salt and pepper and toss to combine. Serve with the remaining half lemon for those who want to squeeze on a little extra.

BROCCOLI DI RAPE

Stronger in flavor than the conventional broccoli, if cooked properly, the bitter flavor is unusual and satisfying. It is delicious served with grilled Italian sausages and crusty bread.

1 bunch broccoli rabe
1½ cups best-quality store-bought chicken stock, or use homemade if you have
⅛ teaspoon red pepper flakes
½ teaspoon coarse salt
2 tablespoons extra-virgin olive oil

■ Trim the ends from the broccoli rabe and cut the remaining stalks crosswise into ¾-inch pieces at the floret end and thinly at the stem end. Float in a bowl of cold water, drain and repeat.

■ In a large pot with a tight-fitting lid, combine the chicken stock and red pepper flakes and bring to a boil. Add salt to taste—some canned broth is saltier than others. Add the broccoli rabe to the pot and cover. Reduce the heat to low and simmer for 10 minutes. Serve in bowls topped with drizzled olive oil.

POMODORO SALAD

MAKES 4 TO 6 SERVINGS

Along with baked artichokes and meatball sandwiches, this tomato salad was instituted into our daily repertoire by Rose, my non-Italian mom, who personalized her favorite recipes of her mother-in-law, our grandmother, Mary Ferlo. Nowadays all my brothers make this and it is always on Rose's table in the summer during peak tomato season. You will need plenty of fresh crusty bread to sop up the "sugo." You may use this same recipe but dice the tomatoes for a quick sauce or relish.

4 fresh ripe tomatoes
1 teaspoon coarse salt
1 small red onion, sliced thinly length-wise
   (about ½ cup)
¼ cup chopped fresh flat-leaf parsley
2 cloves garlic, minced
2 tablespoons torn fresh basil leaves
½ teaspoon fresh thyme or oregano, or
   ¼ teaspoon dried
3 tablespoons extra-virgin olive oil
1 loaf fresh whole bread, torn in pieces

■ Bring a small pot of water to a boil. Submerge each tomato for 10 seconds each and immediately run under cold water. The skin should easily peel off. Cut out the core, slice into thin wedges and place in a medium-size bowl. Add the salt and mix.

■ Add the onion, parsley, garlic, basil, thyme or oregano and olive oil. Stir until well combined. Chill until ready to serve, preferably at least 30 minutes. Serve in salad bowls with hunks of bread on the side.

ARUGULA SALAD WITH SHAVED PARMESAN

MAKES 4 TO 6 SERVINGS

This is another classic and refreshing simple salad, which you can improvise on depending on your personal taste. I love it as is, served after the main course at supper. It makes an excellent light lunch topped with grilled shrimp and white beans or piled high on top of Chicken Milanese (page 90) or plain pizza.

1 bunch arugula, ends trimmed, cleaned well and completely dried
½ cup thinly sliced red onion
⅓ cup extra-virgin olive oil, plus more for serving
2 tablespoons fresh lemon juice
½ teaspoon coarse salt
Freshly ground black pepper
12 to 16 long, thin slices Parmesan cheese

Tear the large arugula leaves in half and place all the leaves into a salad bowl. Add the red onion and toss to combine.

In a small bowl, whisk together the olive oil, lemon juice, salt and pepper. Pour over the salad a little at a time until it is lightly coated. Divide the salad onto chilled salad plates. Top each plate with several slices of Parmesan cheese. Drizzle with olive oil and grind more pepper over. Serve immediately.

LUCA'S CAESAR SALAD

MAKES 4 TO 6 SERVINGS

This is the favorite salad of my salad-loving third-born son. He wholeheartedly approved of this version of my grandmother's recipe made without anchovies. But, by all means, top the salad with anchovies if you please. The lettuce should be fresh and well cleaned. Float the lettuce in a bowl of cold water, drain and repeat. Spin dry and layer the lettuce on a clean towel, topped with paper towel and layered again. Roll up the towel and place in the refrigerator until ready to use. This makes the coldest and crispest lettuce, which is most important for this salad.

¾ cup extra-virgin olive oil
2 cloves garlic, crushed
2 cups fresh bread cubes, crusts removed and cut ¾-inch square
1 teaspoon coarse salt
2 heads romaine lettuce, blemished outer leaves removed and discarded, cleaned as directed above and cut crosswise into 1-inch strips (about 6 cups)
2 large eggs, soft-cooked for 2½ minutes in boiling water
3 tablespoons fresh lemon juice
½ cup freshly grated Parmesan cheese
Freshly ground black pepper
Anchovies (optional)

■ At least 15 minutes and up to several hours in advance, in a small bowl, combine ½ cup of the olive oil and the garlic and set aside.

■ When ready to cook, heat the garlic oil in a large skillet over medium-high heat. Add the bread cubes and cook, stirring, until golden brown, 2 to 3 minutes. Drain on paper towel and toss with ¼ teaspoon of the salt.

■ Place the cold lettuce in a salad bowl. Pour the remaining ¼ cup of olive oil over the lettuce. Add the remaining ¾ teaspoon of salt and toss well. Place the shelled, whole eggs in the center of the lettuce. Add the lemon juice and toss well. The soft-cooked eggs will break apart and combine with the lemon juice to coat the salad with creamy dressing. Add Parmesan cheese and toasted bread cubes, toss again and top with pepper. Top with anchovies, if desired, and serve immediately.

SOUP PIZZA AND SAVORY PIES

MINESTRONE

Minestrone, a thick vegetable soup, is prepared in many delicious varieties but few of them resemble the heavy tomato/pasta soups many of us are used here. I love to make soup for the family, preparing it in the morning. The flavor develops and there is a hearty meal for lunch or dinner. This meatless recipe is a baseline to work from; you should add your favorite vegetables and make it your own. Be mindful to vary the cut and size of your vegetables so they all stand out. A leftover rind from a piece of Parmigiano-Reggiano cheese adds that important rich flavor usually achieved from a meat stock. You may also stir in some fresh Pesto (page 46) just before serving to add an additional dimension to the soup.

4 tablespoons extra-virgin olive oil, plus more for drizzling
1 onion, chopped (about 1½ cups)
3 cloves garlic, minced
4 small zucchini, trimmed and quartered lengthwise, chopped into ½-inch pieces
3 celery stalks (the tender inner stalks with leaves), sliced crosswise into ¼-inch slices
1 small head cauliflower, cored, florets removed and separated into bite-sized pieces
6 ounces green beans, sliced in ¾-inch pieces (about 1 cup)
1 small head cabbage, cored, outer leaves discarded and thinly sliced
16 ounces fresh or canned tomatoes, chopped (about 2 cups)
2 tablespoons coarse salt
½ teaspoon freshly ground black pepper, plus more for serving
1 rind of Parmesan cheese (optional)
1½ cups cooked chickpeas, or 1 (15-ounce) can, rinsed and drained
2 large whole basil sprigs
Freshly grated Parmesan cheese

■ Place 2 tablespoons of the olive oil, the onion and garlic in a large heavy-bottomed, soup pot over medium heat. Cook slowly, stirring occasionally, until the onion is translucent, about 3 minutes. Add the zucchini and the celery and keep cooking, stirring occasionally, for 2 minutes more. Add another tablespoon of the olive oil and the cauliflower and cook 5 minutes, stirring occasionally, as the vegetables slowly begin to soften. Stir in the green beans, cabbage, and remaining olive oil, and cook, stirring occasionally, for another 2 minutes. Stir in the tomatoes and 2 cups water and simmer until all of the vegetables are softened, 5 to 8 minutes more.

■ Add the salt, pepper and Parmesan cheese rind and stir. Add more water if needed for the desired consistency—it should be very thick. Cover and simmer 30 minutes. Add the chickpeas and basil sprigs and cook until the chickpeas are heated through, 5 to 6 minutes. Serve in bowls with Parmesan cheese grated over top, freshly ground pepper and drizzled with olive oil.

CANNELLINI BEAN SOUP

I grew up eating a soup referred to only as "minestra" made of chicken broth, red beans and spinach. Minestra is really just the Italian word for soup—used by the Italian Americans to describe their family's soup. Anyway, I just adore bean soups and nowhere are they more delicious than in Tuscany where the term *manga fagiola,* or "bean eaters," refers to the important role this dietary staple plays in their culture. I've enjoyed many delicious bean soups on my visits in Italy. I developed this recipe to showcase the incredible bean flavor of some imported heirloom beans I received from my Tuscan friend. This soup only tastes better if made a day ahead making it perfect for do-ahead entertaining.

2¾ cups dry cannellini beans
3 tablespoons extra-virgin olive oil, plus more for drizzling
2 onions, chopped (about 2 cups)
3 cloves garlic, minced
5 small (6-inch-long) carrots, peeled, halved lengthwise and sliced (about 1¼ cups)
4 celery stalks (the tender inner stalks with leaves), peeled and chopped (about 1¼ cups)
½ cup chopped tomatoes, fresh or canned
¼ cup fresh basil leaves
¼ cup chopped fresh flat-leaf parsley
1 tablespoon coarse salt
Freshly grated Parmesan cheese
Freshly ground black pepper

■ Rinse the beans well and place in a large pot. Cover the beans with 4 quarts of water. Bring to a boil, cover and turn off the heat. Allow to soak for 1 hour.

■ Place the olive oil, onions and garlic in a large heavy-bottomed pot over medium heat. When the garlic begins to sizzle, after about 30 seconds, add the carrots and celery and continue to cook, stirring, for about 5 minutes. Stir in the tomatoes, basil and parsley and cook, stirring occasionally, for an additional 3 minutes.

■ Add 6 cups of the soaked beans, cover with 10 cups of cold water and stir to combine. Bring to a boil, reduce the heat and simmer, partially covered, until the beans are tender and creamy, at least 1½ but up to 2½ hours. Add water if necessary to achieve desired consistency; the soup should be thick. Add the salt halfway through the cooking. Serve with freshly grated Parmesan cheese and freshly black pepper and a drizzle of olive oil.

STRACCIATELLA SOUP

MAKES 4 SERVINGS

If my brothers and I were ever sick growing up, this is the food we were given to eat. It was cozy and tasty and a way to deliver that important medicine, chicken broth. We called it rag soup because when the eggs and cheese are poured into the hot broth, it resembles raggedy rags. I added the spinach and garlic just to make it even healthier.

4 cups (32 ounces) best-quality chicken broth
3 large eggs
⅓ cup freshly grated Parmesan cheese
1 tablespoon chopped fresh flat-leaf parsley
¼ teaspoon coarse salt
⅛ teaspoon freshly ground black pepper
4 ounces fresh spinach
1 clove garlic, minced

■ Heat the chicken broth to boiling in a medium-size saucepan.

■ In a small bowl, beat the eggs together and stir in the cheese, parsley, salt and pepper. Slowly, in a steady stream, pour the egg mixture into the boiling broth. Stir slightly. Reduce the heat to medium and let cook for 1 minute. Drop the spinach into the broth to wilt. Stir in the garlic. Serve immediately.

BASIC PIZZA DOUGH

MAKES 6 INDIVIDUAL 6-INCH PIZZAS

Eating pizza in Italy or in one of the fine artisanal pizza parlors around our country has to be one of life's great culinary pleasures. But, pizza making at home is so easy and it allows for everyone to personalize his or her own favorite pies.

This crust is how I like it—thin, cracker-like and slightly chewy. The dough may be prepared ahead, the night before, and left to slowly rise in the refrigerator, which will also develop a better flavor and texture. My personal favorite pizzas are a Margherita with an arugula salad (page 80) piled on top of the cooked pie or with the escarole topping on page 83. When we visited Nonny she'd line the kids up in the kitchen with a handful of pizza dough each to make what we called "pizza frizza." We'd shape it our own way and she'd fry it, drain and sprinkle sugar on top.

½ cup water
½ cup milk
1 package dry yeast (2½ teaspoons)
¼ teaspoon sugar
1 tablespoon extra-virgin olive oil, plus more for brushing
2½ cups all-purpose flour, plus more for kneading
2 teaspoons coarse salt

■ Heat the water and milk in a small saucepan over low heat until lukewarm, about 40 seconds. Transfer to a large bowl. Sprinkle the yeast and sugar over the liquid and stir. Let sit until the yeast is dissolved, up to 5 minutes.

■ Stir in the olive oil, flour and salt. Once the dough is combined, knead on a lightly-floured surface until the dough is smooth and elastic, 10 to 15 minutes.

■ Brush a large bowl with olive oil. Add the dough and lightly brush the top with olive oil. Cover and let stand in a warm place until doubled in size, about 3 hours. Or, place in the refrigerator overnight to rise slowly. Punch the dough down and divide into the appropriate number of pizzas, as directed in the recipes that follow. Place the dough balls on a baking sheet and cover until ready to roll out.

PIZZA MARGHERITA

MAKES SIX 6-INCH INDIVIDUAL PIZZAS

This basic Neapolitan-style pizza, Margherita, is perfect as is. When there is a household of kids, I can't keep these coming out of the oven fast enough.

Folks can also create their own personal pie on top of this basic formula, if you prepare bowls of your favorite thin-sliced vegetables, meats and cheeses to choose from. The homemade pizza we ate growing up was a large rectangle pie, topped only with sauce and freshly grated Parmesan. To make, divide the dough in half and roll it out into two rectangle shapes. Proceed as directed omitting the mozzarella and basil and sprinkling with freshly grated Parmesan instead.

1 recipe Basic Pizza Dough (page 79),
  divided into 6 pieces
⅓ cup yellow cornmeal
2 tablespoons extra-virgin olive oil
1 recipe Pomodoro sauce (page 41), or
  other basic tomato sauce
1 pound fresh mozzarella, sliced thin
36 fresh basil leaves, washed and dried

■ Preheat the oven to 450°F. Put the oven rack in the upper part of the oven. Place a pizza stone or heavy-bottomed baking sheet in the oven to preheat.

■ On a clean work surface, roll out the dough pieces to about 6 inches round and ¼ inch thick. Pick up the dough and stretch further with your fingers. Prepare as many pies as will fit on the stone or baking sheet at one time. Spread some cornmeal on a large wooden pizza peel. Place the rolled dough on the wooden peel one at a time.

■ Lightly brush the entire pie with olive oil. Thinly spread 2 to 3 tablespoons of Pomodoro sauce around the pie, leaving a ½-inch border of dough around the pie. Place 4 slices of cheese evenly around the pie. Lay on 4 to 6 basil leaves. Add other toppings, if desired, at this point.

■ Open the oven and pull out the oven rack. Working quickly, slide the pie with the flick of the wrist on to the hot stone or pan. Cook the pizza for 10 to 15 minutes, until the crust is golden and the cheese melted and bubbling. Serve immediately and repeat with the remaining pies.

ESCAROLE PIZZA

MAKES TWO 10-INCH PIZZAS

This is one of the most versatile and delicious recipes in this book. It can be used to top a pizza, it can be tossed with a pound of pasta, or it can even be eaten as a side dish. The flavors combine in concert with escarole to achieve a unique and addictive taste. Escarole is widely available in most supermarkets yet many people, who are unfamiliar with it, only regard it as a bitter lettuce. But cooked, it is very mellow and friendly. Even try it as a relish for grilled pork chops. No one could pick out the addition of anchovies here unless told. A few anchovies added at the beginning of many recipes simply create a rich bottom flavor, which isn't fishy at all.

2 tablespoons extra-virgin olive oil
2 tablespoons best-quality salt-cured anchovies
3 tablespoons chopped black olives such as Gaeta or Niçoise
1 tablespoon small capers, well rinsed
¼ to ½ teaspoon red pepper flakes (to taste)
1 bunch fresh escarole, sliced ¾ inch crosswise and washed, with water still clinging to the leaves (about 8 cups)
⅓ cup freshly grated Parmesan cheese
1 recipe Basic Pizza Dough (page 79), divided into 6 pieces
⅓ cup yellow cornmeal

■ In a large skillet, heat the olive oil over medium-high heat. Add the anchovies and cook, stirring, until they dissolve into a paste, 30 to 60 seconds. Stir in the olives, capers and red pepper flakes and cook, stirring, until the flavors are well combined, 2 to 3 minutes.

■ Reduce the heat to medium and add the escarole to the pan, little by little as the leaves will quickly wilt and make room for more. Cook over medium heat, stirring often, until tender, 5 to 8 minutes.

■ To prepare the pizza, proceed as directed in the previous recipe, but omit the sauce, mozzarella and basil. Instead, spread a thin layer of the escarole and grated Parmesan cheese over the dough and bake.

SPINACH AND HAM PIE

MAKES 6 TO 8 SERVINGS

We cooked this pie at my very first cooking job when I was a teenager. It is an anglicized version of a savory ricotta and Swiss chard pie I've since enjoyed in Italy. Still this is the pie I serve at Easter brunch; it's so good with the crackery-flavored crust and served with a cool and crispy salad. It is also delicious without the ham.

8 tablespoons (1 stick) unsalted butter, at room temperature
4 ounces cream cheese, at room temperature
¼ cup heavy cream
1½ cups plus 2 tablespoons all-purpose flour, plus more for rolling
3 teaspoons coarse salt
3 (10-ounce) packages fresh spinach, stemmed and washed well, with water still clinging to the leaves
3 tablespoons extra-virgin olive oil
1 onion, finely chopped
1 pound fresh ricotta cheese
½ cup freshly grated Parmesan cheese
3 large eggs, lightly beaten (1 reserved for egg wash)
½ teaspoon freshly ground black pepper
8 ounces best-quality ham, cut in ¼-inch cubes (optional)

■ To make the pastry, combine the butter and cream cheese in a food processor or standing mixer. Process until combined. Add the cream and process until combined. Add the flour and 1½ teaspoon of the salt and process until just combined and a ball forms. Turn it out onto a floured surface, divide into 2 pieces and form into discs. Cover in plastic wrap and refrigerate for at least 30 minutes.

■ Meanwhile, preheat the oven to 350°F.

■ Place the spinach in a large pot over medium-high heat. Cover and cook, stirring occasionally, until all the leaves are wilted, 4 to 5 minutes. Remove from the pot and set in a colander to drain until cooled. Squeeze it dry and chop; you should have 2 cups.

■ Meanwhile, place the olive oil and onion in a medium-size skillet over medium heat. Cook, stirring, until the onion is translucent, about 4 minutes. Cool slightly.

■ In a large bowl, combine the ricotta cheese, Parmesan cheese, 2 of the eggs, 1½ teaspoons of the remaining salt and the pepper. Stir in the spinach, onion and ham, if desired.

■ On a lightly floured surface, roll out 1 piece of dough to fit a 9-inch pie plate. Trim the dough edge to hang ¼ inch over the sides. Spread the spinach mixture evenly over dough. Roll out the second piece of dough and drape over the spinach. Trim the dough to hang over the bottom crust by ½ inch. Fold the top crust over and inside the bottom. Using your fingers, crimp the dough to seal. Cut a few vents in the top. Beat the remaining egg with a little water and brush lightly over the pie. Bake the pie for 1 hour or until it is golden brown. Let rest for 15 minutes before cutting and serving.

POLENTA

This recipe makes a soft and loose polenta, which I love to serve with Pork Chops with Vinegar Sauce (page 94). Topped with Sautéed Mushrooms (page 61), it makes a great, light vegetarian dish or appetizer. The polenta can also be placed in a shallow dish to firm it up. It can then be cut in squares, fried in olive oil and served with your morning eggs. To cut back on a little time, there are excellent quick-cooking polentas available at the market now. Follow the directions below, but cook it for the length of time recommended on the package.

4 cups water
1 cup heavy cream
3 tablespoons unsalted butter
1 teaspoon coarse salt
1 cup polenta (stone-ground yellow cornmeal)
½ cup freshly grated Parmesan cheese
2 tablespoons mixed fresh herbs, finely
  chopped (optional)
Freshly ground black pepper

In a medium saucepan, bring 4 cups water and cream to a boil. Add 2 tablespoons of the butter and the salt. Slowly stir in the polenta, reduce the heat to a simmer and cook, stirring constantly, until thick and creamy, 15 to 20 minutes. Stir in the cheese, optional herbs, pepper and remaining tablespoon of butter. Serve immediately or spread in a baking dish to firm up (see Headnote).

RISOTTO MILANESE

Once you get the hang of making risotto, the variations are infinite. Milanese-style is a famous classic distinguished by its saffron flavor. This cooking technique, little by little stirring hot stock into sautéed rice, results in a creamy texture, yet still the grains are separate and toothsome. Serve as you would any rice dish but it is a typical accompaniment for Osso Buco (page 99).

5 to 6 cups best-quality low-sodium beef stock, or chicken stock can be substituted
1 teaspoon coarse salt
2 tablespoons unsalted butter
2 tablespoons extra-virgin olive oil
1 small onion, finely chopped (about ½ cup)
2 cups Arborio Italian rice
¾ cup dry white wine
3 tablespoons heavy cream
¼ teaspoon chopped saffron threads, dissolved in ¼ cup of hot broth
⅓ cup freshly grated Parmesan cheese

■ Place the stock and salt in a 2-quart saucepan and heat until just under boiling.

■ In a large pot over medium heat, melt 1 tablespoon of the butter with the olive oil and heat until bubbling. Add the onion and cook, stirring constantly, until transparent, 2 to 3 minutes. Raise the heat, stir in the rice and cook until it is opaque and slightly sticky, about 2 minutes.

■ Stir in the wine until it is absorbed. Slowly stir in the stock, ½ cup at a time, stirring continually, until the stock is almost completely absorbed before adding more to repeat the process until done. The total cooking time, once all the stock has been stirred in, should be about 18 minutes, but begin testing after 14 minutes for doneness. The rice should be tender yet still firm. Stir in the cream and saffron.

■ Turn off the heat and stir in the remaining tablespoon of butter and the Parmesan cheese. Serve immediately.

CHICKEN
MEAT
AND
FISH

CHICKEN MILANESE

MAKES 6 SERVINGS

I learned this recipe from a Neopolitan who learned it from a Milanese chef. This is one of the most popular recipes I've ever given out to friends. It is distinguished by two techniques. First, the boneless breast is butterflied rather than pounded thin, which keeps it more tender. Second, the breast is "marinated," not just dipped, in eggs—preferably for a long time. For a family meal, I'd offer a bowl of Spaghetti Pomodoro (page 41), followed by this chicken and a side of spinach. It is also excellent served with Pomodoro Salad, drained (page 68), or the Arugula Salad with Shaved Parmesan (page 79) placed right on top.

3 pounds boneless, skinless chicken breasts
4 large eggs, beaten
1 day-old loaf of bread, crusts removed and processed into 1½ cups of breadcrumbs
1 teaspoon coarse salt, plus more for serving
¼ teaspoon freshly ground black pepper, plus more for serving
4 tablespoons (½ stick) unsalted butter
2 tablespoons extra-virgin olive oil
2 lemons, cut into 6 wedges

■ Separate the chicken into individual breasts. Butterfly the breasts by cutting into the center but not completely through, until, when opened, the breast lays flat. Place the butterflied chicken breasts in a large rectangular baking dish. Pour in the eggs and completely coat the chicken. Cover and let stand in the refrigerator for at least 1 hour but up to 12. Periodically rotate the chicken breasts in the egg mixture.

■ Put the breadcrumbs on a large plate and mix in the salt and pepper. One by one remove the chicken breasts from the eggs and lightly coat both sides in the breadcrumbs. Place the pieces on a rack while you continue with the remaining chicken breasts.

■ In a large skillet over medium-high heat, melt 2 tablespoons of the butter and 1 tablespoon of the olive oil until bubbling but not browning. You will have to cook the chicken in two batches. Lay half of the chicken breasts in the pan, without crowding, and cook until golden brown, 3 to 5 minutes. Turn the chicken over and cook 3 to 5 minutes more. Transfer the chicken to a baking sheet and keep warm in the oven while you cook the second batch in the remaining 2 tablespoons of butter and tablespoon of olive oil.

■ Serve the chicken with a wedge of lemon and a sprinkling of salt and pepper.

ROAST CHICKEN WITH HERBS

MAKES 6 TO 8 SERVINGS

Every culture and family has their own recipe for roast chicken. Since this is a weekly meal in our home, I always make two chickens at once, so I'm sure to have plenty for any last-minute guests or leftovers for sandwiches the next day. Invest in the best, most naturally raised chicken possible, as it will reflect the final taste. Anyone who's eaten the chicken and eggs in Italy knows—they still manage to produce and sell tasty well-fed chickens.

4 tablespoons fresh rosemary leaves, or 2 tablespoons dried

6 to 8 fresh sage leaves, depending on size, or 3 to 4 dried

2 tablespoons fresh marjoram leaves, or 1 tablespoon dried

1 tablespoon fresh thyme leaves, or 1½ teaspoons dried

1 tablespoon minced fresh chives

2 bay leaves

1 tablespoon caraway seeds

2 lemons, juiced (8 tablespoons), rinds reserved

2 tablespoons olive oil

1½ teaspoons coarse salt

½ teaspoon freshly ground black pepper

2 (3-pound) whole chickens

■ Place the rosemary, sage, marjoram, thyme, chives, bay leaves and caraway on a chopping board. Chop everything together to achieve a uniform texture. In a small bowl, combine the herbs with 2 tablespoons of the lemon juice, the olive oil, ½ teaspoon of the salt and ¼ teaspoon of the pepper. Set aside.

■ Clean the birds very thoroughly inside and out and dry all over with paper towels. Pour 3 tablespoons of the lemon juice over each chicken and inside the cavity. Rub the herb mixture all over the inside and outside of both birds. Place the reserved lemon rinds inside the cavities. Let the birds marinate in the refrigerator for at least 1 hour or up to 12.

■ Preheat the oven to 450°F.

■ Sprinkle the remaining teaspoon of salt and ¼ teaspoon of pepper over both birds. Place the birds, breast side down, side by side, in opposite directions on an oiled rack over a roasting pan. Cook for 30 minutes, then turn the chickens breast side up and reduce the heat to 375°F. Cook an additional 30 to 40 minutes or until the skin is golden, juices run clear and the internal temperature is 160°F. Allow the birds to rest for 15 to 20 minutes before carving and serving.

PORK CHOPS WITH VINEGAR SAUCE

MAKES 4 SERVINGS

The technique for this recipe is also delicious when used on chicken pieces, especially thighs. Choose thick-cut pork chops and serve this with the Polenta (page 87) and one of the hearty greens like Tuscan Kale (page 60).

½ cup red wine vinegar
4 cloves garlic, 2 minced, 2 left whole
3 tablespoons rosemary leaves, or 1½
   tablespoons dried
4 (1-inch-thick) center cut pork chops
Coarse salt
Freshly ground black pepper

In a small bowl, combine the vinegar, garlic and rosemary. Set aside for at least 15 minutes or up to several hours.

Preheat the oven to 375°F.

Season both sides of the pork chops with salt and pepper. Heat a large ovenproof skillet over high heat until it is very hot. Add the pork chops to the pan, working in batches if necessary to avoid crowding the pan. Cook 3 minutes per side and don't move the chops until ready to turn. Transfer the skillet to the oven for 15 minutes.

Carefully remove the pan from the oven and return to the stovetop over high heat. Pour in the vinegar mixture and swirl it around in the pan, turn the chops to coat them in the sauce on both sides, and cook until the sauce has a syrupy consistency and the internal temperature of the chops is 140°F, about 4 minutes. If necessary, remove the chops to a warm platter to reduce the liquid further without overcooking chops, then return the chops to the pan to coat. Serve immediately with a little sauce dribbled on each chop.

BEEF BRACIOLA

MAKES 4 TO 6 SERVINGS

I found several variations on this recipe, another family favorite of my dad, Carmine George Scala, in his mother's recipe file. One, for Brociolette Ripene is rolled with prosciutto, pine nuts, parsley and raisins, which you could also try preparing with ¾ cup of white wine instead of red wine and tomato sauce. For the family purists who know the recipe, I've only made a few changes. I like to serve pasta with the sauce from the beef as a first course and serve the beef with a vegetable for second.

4 tablespoons extra-virgin olive oil, plus
  more for drizzling
3 cloves garlic, minced (about 3 teaspoons)
1½ cups fresh breadcrumbs
½ cup freshly grated Parmesan cheese
¼ cup chopped fresh flat-leaf parsley
1 teaspoon coarse salt
¼ teaspoon freshly ground black pepper
⅛ teaspoon red pepper flakes
½ teaspoon fresh thyme, or ¼ teaspoon
  dried
10 slices top-round sirloin, very thinly
  sliced, pounded to 4 – 6 inches
10 pieces string, 14 inches long
1 small onion, minced
2 tablespoons red wine (optional) or water
1 (28-ounce) can best-quality tomatoes,
  coarsely blended

■ Heat 1 tablespoon of the olive oil and 2 teaspoons of the garlic in a small skillet over medium heat until it sizzles but not browns, about 30 seconds. Stir in the breadcrumbs, remove from the heat and set aside to cool. Stir in the Parmesan, parsley, ½ teaspoon of the salt, ⅛ teaspoon of the black pepper, the red pepper flakes and thyme.

■ Lay the meat out side by side on a clean workspace. Sprinkle each slice with the remaining ½ teaspoon of salt and ⅛ teaspoon black pepper. Place a scant ¼ cup filling over each meat slice, leaving a ¼-inch border. Drizzle on olive oil and roll each piece up from the widest to narrowest end. Tie each piece with the string.

■ Place the remaining 3 tablespoons of the olive oil in a heavy-bottomed skillet over high heat. Just before the oil smokes, add the meat bundles. (Do not crowd the pan or the meat won't brown.) Working in batches if necessary, cook for 2 to 3 minutes per side. Remove the braciola from the pan and keep warm in the oven.

■ Reduce the heat to medium, stir in the onion and the remaining teaspoon of garlic and cook, stirring, for 1 minute. Pour in the wine or water, stirring to deglaze the pan, loosening all the brown bits on the bottom of the pan.

■ Add the tomatoes and bring to a boil. Return the beef to the pan, reduce the heat and simmer, partially covered, for 1 hour. Remove the bundles from the pan, one at a time, snip off the string and return to the pan. The dish may be made a couple days ahead to this point and the taste will improve. Serve as desired.

OSSO BUCO

My Milanese friend taught me this essential version of Osso Buco. I serve this dish for special occasions accompanied with Risotto Milanese (page 88) served as a first course. It is simple to prepare but when cooked properly, an absolutely delicious treat. The veal shanks are usually sold very thick but I prefer them cut about ¾ inch thick so ask your butcher for a special cut or prepare to cook them longer. It is topped with the authentic gremolata garnish.

6 pieces veal shank, cut about ¾ inch thick
Coarse salt
Freshly ground black pepper
¼ cup all-purpose flour, preferably Wondra
2 tablespoons extra-virgin olive oil
2 tablespoons unsalted butter
2½ cups best-quality Italian white wine
3 tablespoons minced fresh flat-leaf
    parsley
1½ tablespoons minced fresh orange peel
1½ tablespoons minced fresh lemon peel
3 cloves garlic, finely minced

░ Generously season both sides of the veal shanks with salt and pepper. Lightly coat in the flour and shake off the excess.

░ Heat a large heavy-bottomed pan over high heat. Add the olive oil and butter and swirl them around the pan. Add the shanks and cook for 3 minutes per side, until golden brown. Add the wine to the pan and stir it occasionally to deglaze the browned bits on the bottom of the pan. Reduce the heat to medium-low, partially cover and simmer for 30 minutes. Turn the meat and cook until tender, about 30 minutes more.

░ Meanwhile, in a small bowl, combine the parsley, orange and lemon peel and garlic. Serve the shanks, topped with a sprinkling of the citrus-parsley mixture.

POLPETTE

MAKES 6 SERVINGS

My Sicilian/Italian/Irish husband, of the Cantisano Quinn family, is the expert meat loaf–maker in our family. This is one of my favorite weeknight family meals served with mashed potatoes mixed with ricotta cheese and butter, which is an amazing combination. We always serve a couple of vegetable dishes, sparkling water and wine at the table too.

⅓ cup milk
1 (1½-inch) slice bread, crust removed
1 pound ground pork
1 pound ground veal or beef
⅓ pound mortadella, minced
1 small onion, finely chopped (about ½ cup)
½ cup chopped fresh flat-leaf parsley
½ cup freshly grated Parmesan cheese
¼ cup pistachio nuts, chopped
2 cloves garlic, minced
2 large eggs, lightly beaten
2 tablespoons white or red wine
½ teaspoon coarse salt
¼ teaspoon freshly ground black pepper

■ Preheat the oven to 400°F.

■ Heat the milk in a small pan until warm but not scalded. Turn off the heat. Place the bread in the milk and let sit to absorb the milk, turning once, about 1 minute per side. Remove the bread to a board, finely chop it and place the bread in a large bowl.

■ Add the pork, veal, mortadella, onion, parsley, cheese, nuts, garlic, eggs, wine, salt and pepper to the bread. Using your hands, mix to combine completely. Form into an oval-shaped loaf and place in a large baking dish. Cook for 55 minutes. Let rest 10 minutes before serving.

VEAL PICCATTA

MAKES 2 SERVINGS

I like to make this dish two servings at a time. Given that good-quality veal is so pricey, I usually only serve it as a treat when I'm cooking for two but you may simply multiply the quantities accordingly for your needs. Lemon is the star here so prepare it for your favorite lemon lover who, in our home, is my mom who loves ALL things lemon. It takes minutes to prepare so have the elements of your meal organized and cook the veal at the last moment.

4 thin-sliced veal scallopini (about ⅔ pound), lightly pounded
Coarse salt
Ground white pepper
2 tablespoons all-purpose flour, preferably Wondra
1 tablespoon extra-virgin olive oil
1 tablespoon unsalted butter
2 tablespoons best-quality white wine, or dry vermouth
1 lemon, half juiced (2 tablespoons), half thinly sliced, crosswise

■ Season the veal on both sides with salt and white pepper. Lightly coat in the flour. Shake off the excess.

■ Heat a large skillet over medium-high heat. Add the olive oil and butter, swirl them around the pan and add the veal. Turn the heat to high and sauté the veal for 1 minute per side. Pour in the wine, swirl it around the pan for 20 seconds and turn over the veal. Add the lemon juice and slices, swirl them around in the pan and turn off the heat. Serve immediately with a small sprinkling of salt and white pepper.

FISH FILLET WITH ROSEMARY

MAKES 2 SERVINGS

A couple of years ago, I ate fish at a local New York Italian restaurant that I couldn't stop thinking about once I'd left, which is a sure sign of a well-executed dish. This is my best guess as to how it was made. It is a great fish recipe for anyone who thinks they don't like fish; the mild fillet serves as a vehicle for the herbaceous and earthy flavors of the sauce. You may use any firm-fleshed white fish fillet such as red snapper, sea bass or even fresh sea scallops. For an alternative cooking method, you could place all the ingredients (without flouring) in a parchment or foil pouch and bake in the oven.

I love to serve this with simple boiled potatoes or as a second course after Linguine with Clams (page 55).

1 pound skinless white fish fillet such as red snapper or sea bass, cut into 6- to 8-ounce fillets, about ¾ inch thick (if your fillets are thinner, lessen cooking time)
Coarse salt
Freshly ground black pepper
3 tablespoons all-purpose flour, preferably Wondra
1½ tablespoons extra-virgin olive oil
1 clove garlic, minced (about 1 tablespoon)
¼ cup Italian white wine, or dry vermouth
2 tablespoons pitted black olives, sliced, such as Gaeta or Niçoise
2 teaspoons fresh rosemary leaves, plus 2 sprigs for garnish
1 tablespoon unsalted butter
1 lemon, cut in wedges for garnish

■ Season the fish on both sides with salt and pepper. Lightly dredge it in the flour, shaking off the excess.

■ Heat a medium nonstick skillet over medium-high heat until the pan is very hot. Add the olive oil. Place the fish in the skillet and cook for 2 minutes without moving the fillets. Turn and cook 2 more minutes, reducing heat if necessary to prevent browning. Pour off the fat and flip the fish again.

■ Making room in the side of the pan, add the garlic and cook, stirring, for 10 to 15 seconds, being careful not to let it burn. Immediately add the wine, olives and rosemary leaves and swirl them around in the pan as the wine reduces, about 1½ minutes. Divide the fish between 2 warm serving plates. Swirl the butter into the sauce and pour the sauce evenly over the fish. Garnish with fresh rosemary sprigs and serve with lemon wedges.

GRILLED SHRIMP WITH SALSA VERDE

MAKES 6 SERVINGS

The sauce in this recipe is ubiquitous on the Amalfi coast in southwest Italy where I ate it spooned over a thinly sliced fish steak titled Pesca Spada alla Griglia. It is best enjoyed when the freshest seafood and produce are available. The sauce can be made in advance and the shrimp broiled or grilled just before the meal.

3 cloves garlic
2 tablespoons capers, rinsed and chopped
1 teaspoon coarse salt
1 cup fresh mint leaves, finely chopped
¾ cup chopped fresh flat-leaf parsley
¼ cup extra-virgin olive oil
2 lemons, 1 juiced (2½ tablespoons),
** 1 cut in 6 wedges for garnish**
1 tablespoon red wine vinegar
24 jumbo shrimp, peeled (about 3 pounds)
½ teaspoon freshly ground black pepper

▪ Mince together the garlic, capers and ½ teaspoon of the salt and place in a small bowl. Stir in the mint, parsley, olive oil, lemon juice and red wine vinegar.

▪ Preheat the broiler or prepare a grill. Butterfly the shrimp by slicing down the center of each, lengthwise, almost but not completely through. Open both sides to lay flat. Season with the remaining ½ teaspoon of the salt and the pepper. Broil or grill for 2 minutes per side. Place 4 shrimp on each plate and spoon some of the sauce over.

DESSERTS

AQUALINA'S MOLASSES COOKIES

MAKES 4 DOZEN

No less than ten recipes for molasses cookies exist in Nonny's files, all of which are just slightly different and even include one using warm coffee and lard. The best is titled "mother's favorite," which refers to her mother, Aqualina Spadafore, daughter of Archangela from Calabria, Italy. Aqualina was a formidable woman and way ahead of her time. She received and helped settle many Italian immigrants who came to her hometown, Rome, New York. I remember these cookies on the counter in Nonny's kitchen. Just the smell of them conjures up the exact image of her home in my mind's eye. They have become a favorite of my own family.

3½ cups all-purpose flour
1 teaspoon baking soda
1 teaspoon ground cinnamon
¾ teaspoon coarse salt
½ teaspoon ground ginger
½ teaspoon ground cloves
1 cup light brown sugar
½ cup unsalted butter, melted
½ cup molasses
½ cup whole milk
1 large egg, beaten
1 cup raisins (optional)

■ Preheat the oven to 375°F.

■ In a large bowl, whisk together the flour, baking soda, cinnamon, salt, ginger and cloves. Whisk in the brown sugar. Stir in the butter, molasses, milk and egg. Continue stirring until the dough is well combined. Fold in the raisins, if using.

■ Drop rounded teaspoons of dough onto a parchment-lined baking sheet. Bake for 12 minutes. Remove from the pan onto a wire cooling rack and cool.

CAROLINA'S WINE TARALLI

MAKES 2 ½ DOZEN

My Great-Aunt Carolina Scala, my Grandfather Scala's oldest sister, was well known for her fine cooking as well as her tremendous kindness and grace. These are my dad's favorite cookies, which he remembers with great fondness. He recalls a thin lemon glaze on the cookies, which isn't included in any of the recipes I've found in my grandmother, Mary Scala's old files. Similarly, my mother mentioned observing Aunt Lina (Carolina) boiling the cookie dough before baking, but this isn't mentioned in any of the recipes either. Historically, taralli were typically a savory Italian cookie, which varied from region to region, often enjoyed with wine. However, this recipe is sweet and once again quite different from any taralli I've tasted in Italy. You must leave them to cool completely before storing in an airtight container.

If you wish to ice them, whisk 2 tablespoons of milk and 1 tablespoon of lemon juice into 1 cup confectioners' sugar. It should be the consistency of thick whipping cream. Dip one side of the cookie in the glaze and let dry.

3 cups all-purpose flour
2 teaspoons baking powder
1 teaspoon coarse salt
½ cup sugar
1 large egg
½ cup extra-virgin olive oil
½ cup Marsala wine

■ Preheat the oven to 375°F.

■ In a mixing bowl, whisk together the flour, baking powder and salt.

■ In a separate larger bowl, whisk together the sugar and egg until well combined. Stir in the olive oil and wine. Slowly add the flour mixture until well combined, kneading slightly until the dough is easy to handle and medium-soft.

■ On a clean surface, use your hands and roll the dough into ½-inch-thick, cigar-like rolls. Cut each cigar into 6-inch pieces, folding each piece into a loop-shape. Press the dough with fingers to seal together. Place on a parchment-lined, rimmed baking sheet.

■ Bake for 15 to 20 minutes or until slightly golden. Remove to a cooling rack and cool completely.

ESPRESSO GRANITA

Serve this on a hot summer afternoon as a treat or as a finish to a meal. Topped with a dollop of whipped cream and a few chocolate shavings, it makes a very light and satisfying dessert. This icy dessert utilizes a technique of raking the ice crystals as they form in the freezer, which can be used with citrus juice and many other flavors. We used to go to an Italian shop in Utica, New York, where the kids ate lemon ice while the grown-ups got to have this mysterious treat.

2 cups strong brewed espresso coffee
¼ cup sugar
1 cup water
1 cup heavy whipping cream
8 ounces bittersweet chocolate, shaved into curls (optional)

■ While the coffee is still warm, stir in 3 tablespoons of the sugar until it is dissolved. Blend with the water.

■ Pour the mixture into a 13 x 9-inch Pyrex™ baking dish. Place in the freezer. Every 30 minutes, rake the surface with a fork to dislodge and distribute the ice crystals to form a granular texture. The granita will be ready in 2 hours.

■ Meanwhile, whip the cream with the remaining 1 tablespoon of sugar to form soft peaks.

■ Scoop about 5 ounces of granita into each parfait glass. Top with a dollop of whipped cream and shaved chocolate, if desired. Serve immediately.

MACERATED ORANGES WITH STUFFED DATES AND PISTACHIOS

MAKES 6 SERVINGS

I like simple desserts that satisfy the sweet craving while carrying a little savory essence from the main course. Often, I serve composed desserts, simply placing complementary treats on a large platter such as chocolate, fruits and cheese. Grappa is a favorite after-dinner drink in our family, and I think it adds a unique flavor to the oranges, but if you prefer a different flavor just use another wine or spirit, or omit it all together.

3 oranges, peeled
2 tablespoons grappa
2 teaspoons honey
¾ cup mascarpone cheese
1½ tablespoons sugar
¼ teaspoon cinnamon
¼ teaspoon instant espresso
2 ounces bittersweet chocolate, chopped
12 Medjool dates
1 cup salted pistachio nuts, in the shell

■ Section the oranges by cutting away each section from the membrane. Place in a medium-size serving bowl. Stir in the grappa and honey. Cover and refrigerate until ready to use.

■ In another bowl, mix together the mascarpone, sugar, cinnamon and espresso until well combined. Stir in the chocolate and set aside.

■ Cut a lengthwise slit in each of the dates and remove the pit. Fill each date with ¾ teaspoon of the cheese mixture.

■ Serve the dates and nuts on a platter alongside the bowl of chilled oranges.

ZABAGLIONE WITH FRESH PEACHES AND RASPBERRIES

Zabaglione is the most ethereal light custard, which I like to serve as a sauce over fresh fruit. It must be made at the last minute though, so prepare your fruit, ingredients and equipment before dinner and whip the sauce up just before dessert.

4 peaches
2 large egg yolks
3 tablespoons Marsala wine
2 teaspoons sugar
1 pint raspberries

■ Bring a medium-size pot of water to a boil. Dunk each peach into the boiling water for 10 seconds, then plunge immediately into cold water. Remove the peels—they should come off easily—and slice each peach in half, removing the pits. Set aside.

■ Place a heat-proof bowl over a pot filled with 1 inch of water and bring to a gentle simmer. Add the egg yolks, Marsala wine and sugar and continuously whip until the mixture is creamy and thick, about 4 minutes. Remove from the heat.

■ Arrange the peach halves side by side on a dessert plate and fill with several berries. Spoon the zabaglione sauce over and serve immediately.

INDEX